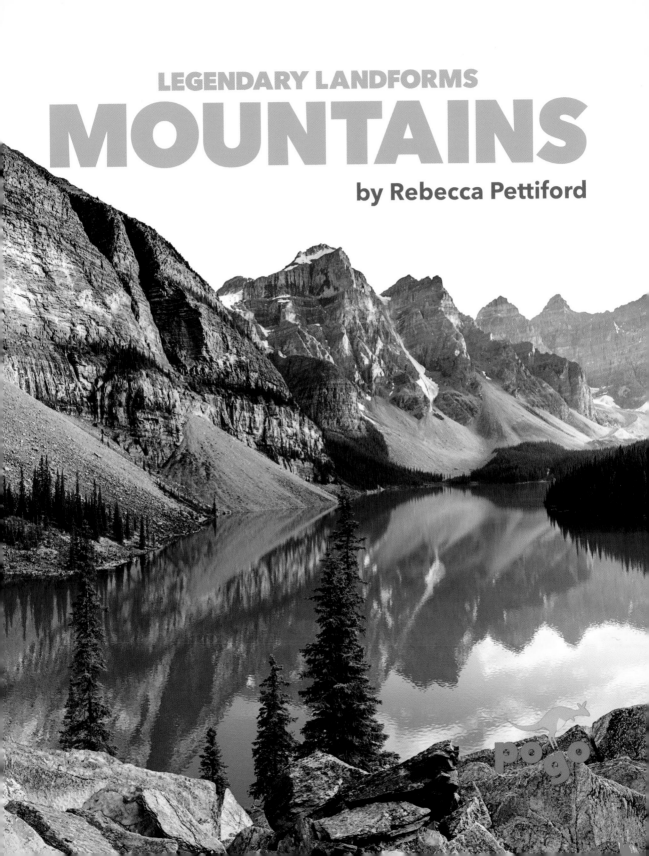

LEGENDARY LANDFORMS
MOUNTAINS

by Rebecca Pettiford

pogo

Ideas for Parents and Teachers

Pogo Books let children practice reading informational text while introducing them to nonfiction features such as headings, labels, sidebars, maps, and diagrams, as well as a table of contents, glossary, and index.

Carefully leveled text with a strong photo match offers early fluent readers the support they need to succeed.

Before Reading

- "Walk" through the book and point out the various nonfiction features. Ask the student what purpose each feature serves.
- Look at the glossary together. Read and discuss the words.

Read the Book

- Have the child read the book independently.
- Invite him or her to list questions that arise from reading.

After Reading

- Discuss the child's questions. Talk about how he or she might find answers to those questions.
- Prompt the child to think more. Ask: Have you ever been to a mountain? Where was it? What kinds of things did you see and do there?

Pogo Books are published by Jump!
5357 Penn Avenue South
Minneapolis, MN 55419
www.jumplibrary.com

Library of Congress Cataloging-in-Publication Data

Names: Pettiford, Rebecca, author.
Title: Mountains / by Rebecca Pettiford.
Description: Minneapolis, MN: Jump!, Inc., [2017]
Series: Legendary landforms | Audience: Ages 7-10.
Includes bibliographical references and index.
Identifiers: LCCN 2016048933 (print)
LCCN 2016050345 (ebook) | ISBN 9781620317082
(hardcover: alk. paper) | ISBN 9781620317464 (pbk.)
ISBN 9781624965852 (ebook)
Subjects: LCSH: Mountains–Juvenile literature.
Landforms–Juvenile literature.
Everest, Mount (China and Nepal)–Juvenile literature.
Classification: LCC GB512 .P47 2017 (print)
LCC GB512 (ebook) | DDC 551.43/2–dc23
LC record available at https://lccn.loc.gov/2016048933

Editor: Kirsten Chang
Book Designer: Leah Sanders
Photo Researcher: Leah Sanders

Photo Credits: Ron_Thomas/Getty, cover; r.classen/Shutterstock, 1; Olga Danylenko/Shutterstock, 3; Harry Hu/Shutterstock, 4; marco wong/Getty, 5; troutnut/Thinkstock, 6-7; DanielPrudek/Thinkstock, 8-9; Philip Rosenberg/Getty, 10-11; Vershinin-M/Thinkstock, 12; Libux77/Dreamstime, 13; Peter Hermes Furian/Shutterstock, 13; WorldWide/Shutterstock, 13; Eduard Moldoveanu/Shutterstock, 14-15; Roger Ressmeyer/Getty, 16-17; Daniel Prudek/Shutterstock, 18-19; hadynyah/iStock, 20-21; Andreas Jung/Shutterstock, 23.

Printed in the United States of America at Corporate Graphics in North Mankato, Minnesota.

TABLE OF CONTENTS

CHAPTER 1

. . . .

TOP OF THE WORLD

All over the world, mountains rise from Earth's surface. These **landforms** are millions of years old.

They have steep, sloping sides. They have sharp or rounded **ridges**. Mountains are taller than hills. They are usually 2,000 feet (610 meters) tall or higher.

The highest point of a mountain is the **summit**. The weather is coolest at the summit. Some mountains have snow on their peaks.

summit

A group of mountains is called a **range**. The Himalayas are a mountain range in Asia. They stretch about 1,500 miles (2,414 kilometers). They pass through six countries. They are home to Mount Everest, the tallest mountain in the world.

DID YOU KNOW?

Yaks. Mountain pumas. Snow leopards. **Ibexes**. These animals have adapted to live in cold mountain regions. They have thick fur to stay warm.

Even the ocean has mountains! Mauna Kea in Hawaii is more than 33,000 feet (10,000 m) high. This actually makes it taller than Everest. However, most mountains are measured above sea level. Most of Mauna Kea is below sea level.

Mauna Kea

CHAPTER 2

BUILDING A MOUNTAIN

Most mountains are formed by the movement of **plates**. These are large pieces of land on Earth's surface. They float on a bed of **molten** rock. They move under and over each other.

Millions of years ago, the plates crashed together. It forced the land up. Mountains formed.

Plates move all the time. This means that mountains are always changing. Even Mount Everest is growing a little each year!

Some mountains are getting smaller. Why? The plates have stopped moving. Over time, **erosion** makes the mountains smaller. This has happened to the Appalachian Mountains in North America. They used to be as tall as the Rocky Mountains. But the Appalachians are much older. Erosion has worn them down over time.

TAKE A LOOK!

How do mountains form?
1 Plates collide.
2 The edges of the plates buckle.
3 Rock is pushed upward. Mountains form.

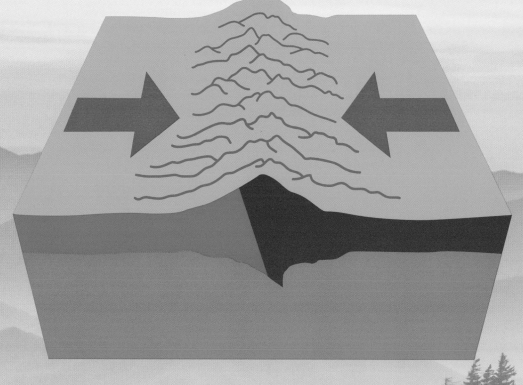

■ = mountains forming   ■ = plate
■ = plate   ■ = molten rock

Volcanoes can form mountains. When they **erupt**, layers of **lava** build up. Over time, a mountain forms. The islands of Hawaii were volcanoes that began under the ocean.

Sometimes, **magma** builds up below Earth's surface. This forces the rocks above it to rise. **Dome mountains** form.

CHAPTER 3

MOUNT EVEREST

Mount Everest is perhaps the most famous mountain in the world. It is in Nepal and Tibet. It is more than 29,000 feet (8,839 m) high.

Mount Everest

It is a **fold mountain**. It formed when two plates crashed together. Layers of rock pushed upward. Then, over millions of years, the layers folded over one another.

Thousands of people have climbed Mount Everest. It takes about two months to reach the summit. Some people have died trying to climb it.

Do you want to climb a mountain closer to home? Be prepared. Wear proper shoes. Drink lots of water. Enjoy these legendary landforms. But don't forget to stay safe!

DID YOU KNOW?

K2 is a mountain in China and Pakistan. For a few weeks in winter, K2 is thought to be taller than Everest. How? Snow gives it more height.

ACTIVITIES & TOOLS

TRY THIS!

MAKE A FOLD MOUNTAIN

Find out how plates on Earth's surface form a fold mountain.

What You Need:
- four cloth placemats of different colors
- two bath towels

1. Stack the four placemats on top of one another so they are flat. These are your rock layers.

2. Fold each bath towel in half lengthwise. Roll each towel up from the short end so it makes a cylinder. The towels act as two plates under the Earth.

3. Place one "plate" at one short end of your stacked placemats (rock layers).

4. Place the other "plate" at the other short end of your rock layers.

5. Using your hands, slowly push the "plates" toward one another.

6. As the plates move, the rock layers rise. They will slowly fold over one another. You have made a fold mountain!

GLOSSARY

dome mountains: Mountains that form when magma builds up under Earth's surface and pushes up rocks.

erosion: The slow destruction of something by water and wind.

erupt: To send out rocks, ash, and lava in a sudden explosion.

fold mountain: A mountain that forms by the contact of Earth's plates; layers of rock fold over one another.

ibexes: Wild goats that live in high mountain areas.

landforms: Natural features of Earth's surface.

lava: Melted rock from a volcano.

magma: Hot liquid rock below Earth's surface.

molten: Melted by a very great heat.

plates: Layers of Earth's crust that move, float, and sometimes fracture.

range: A line or series of mountains or hills.

ridges: Areas of land on top of a mountain or hill.

summit: The highest point of a mountain.

volcanoes: Mountains with a hole in their tops or sides that force out rocks, ash, and lava.

INDEX

TO LEARN MORE

Learning more is as easy as 1, 2, 3.

1) Go to www.factsurfer.com

2) Enter "legendarymountains" into the search box.

3) Click the "Surf" button to see a list of websites.

With factsurfer, finding more information is just a click away.